ELEPHANT
COLORING BOOK
FOR ADULTS

AN ADULT COLORING BOOK OF 40 PATTERNED, HENNA AND PAISLEY STYLE ELEPHANTS

ADULT COLORING WORLD

Copyright © 2015 Adult Coloring World

ISBN-13: 978-1519606594

ISBN-10: 1519606591

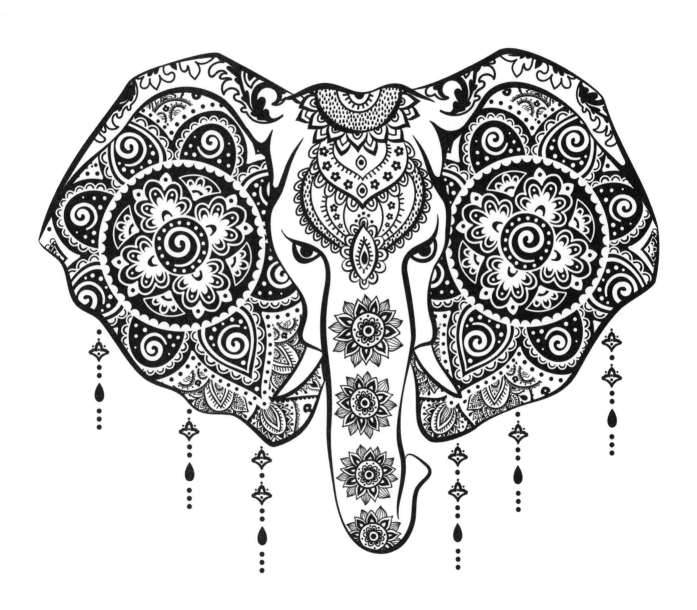

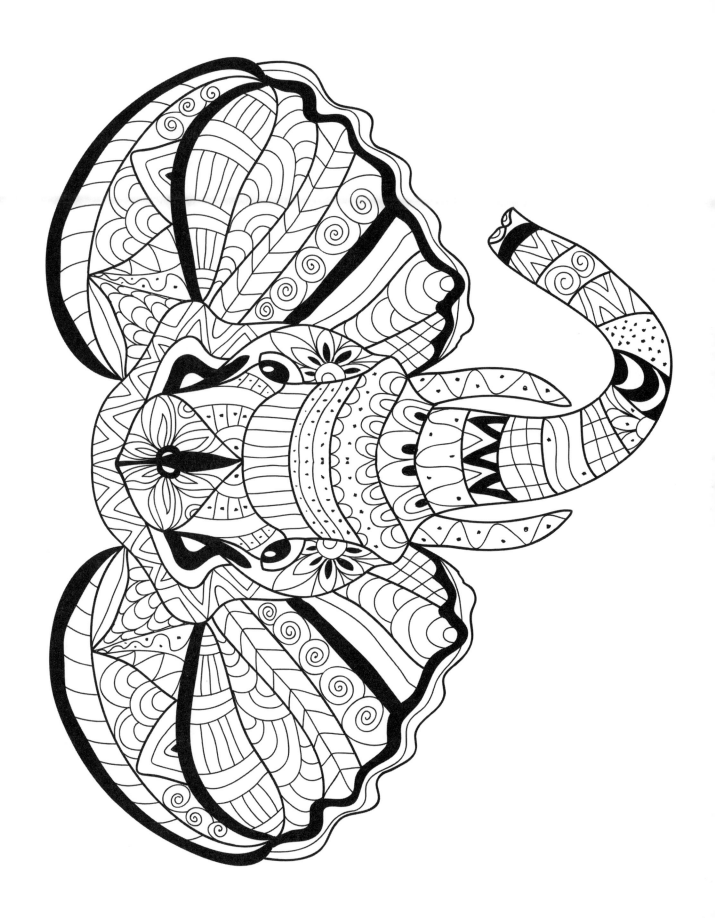

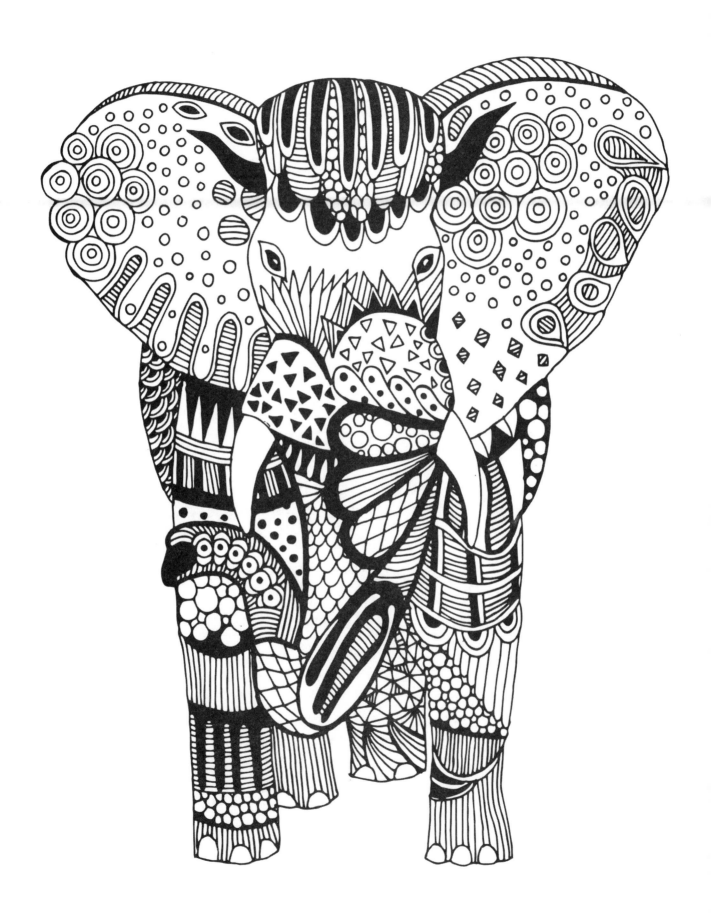

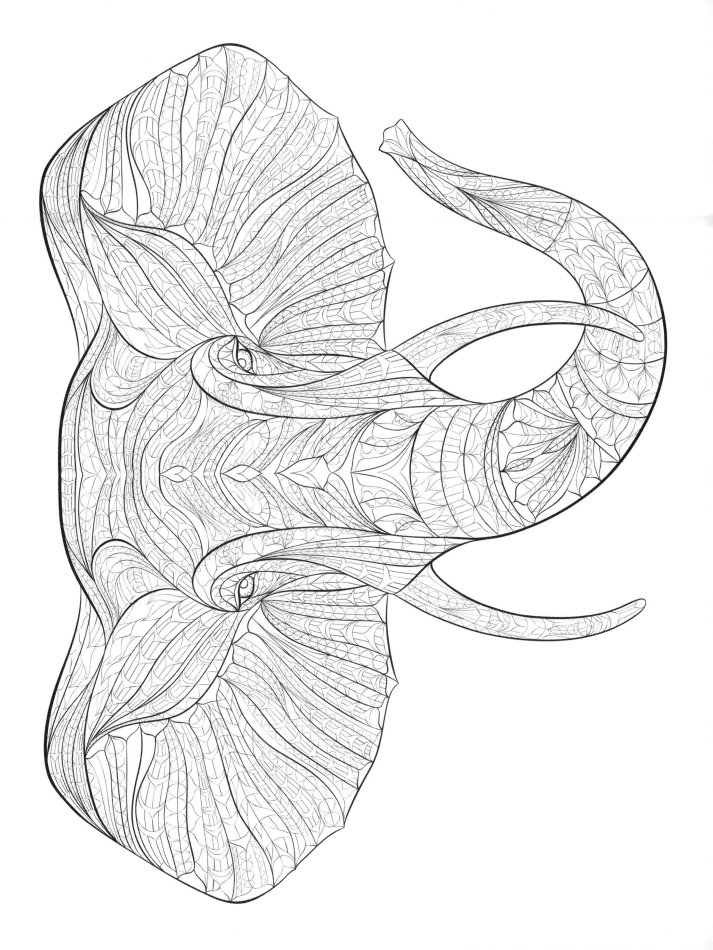

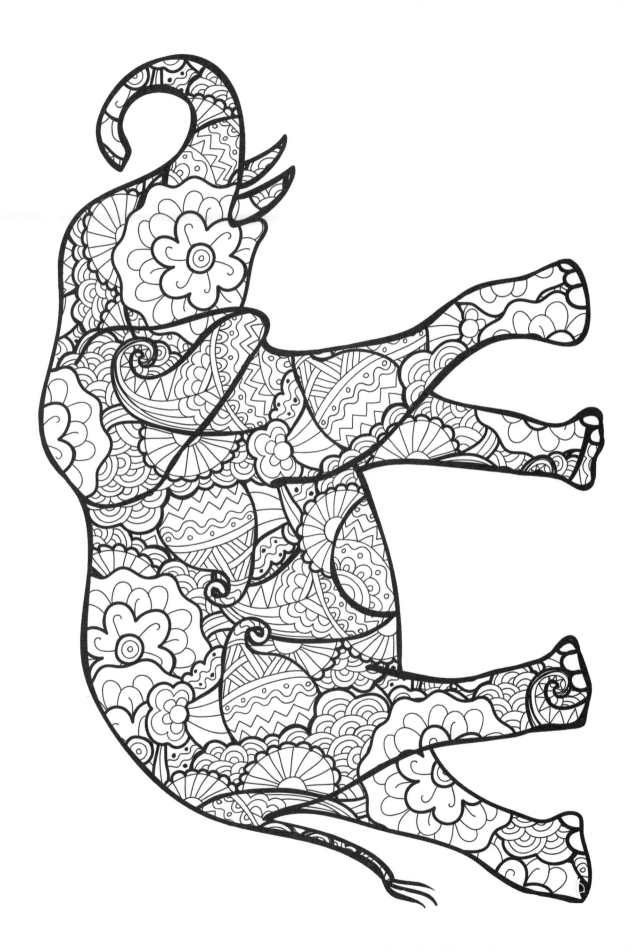

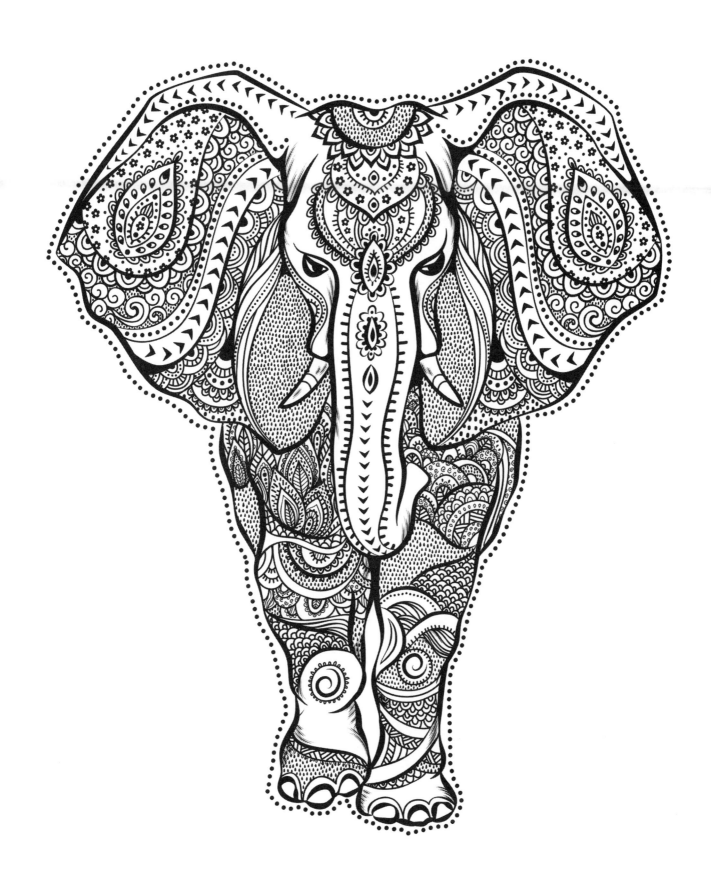

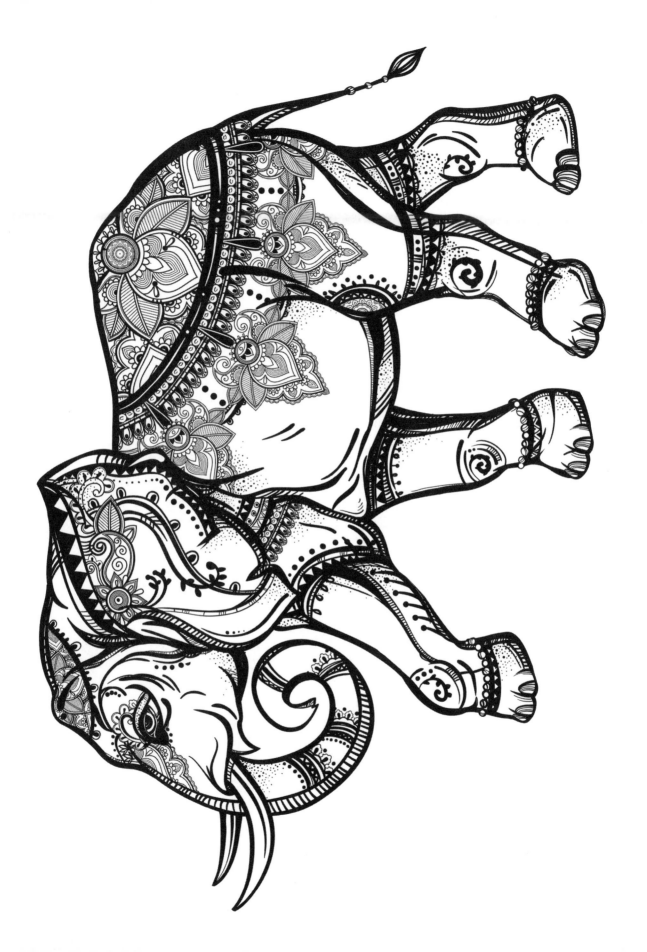

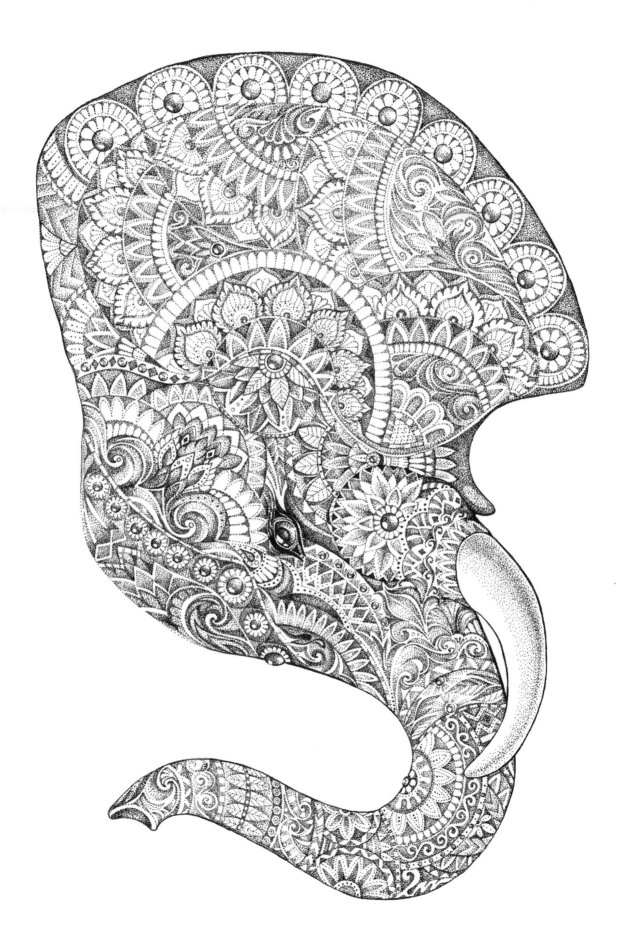